Let's DRAW!

FAVORITE ANIMALS

How2DrawAnimals

Brimming with creative inspiration, how-to projects, and useful information to enrich your everyday life, quarto.com is a favorite destination for those pursuing their interests and passions.

First published in 2022 by Walter Foster Jr., an imprint of The Quarto Group.
100 Cummings Center, Suite 265D, Beverly, MA 01915, USA.
T (978) 282-9590 **F** (978) 283-2742 **www.quarto.com** • **www.walterfoster.com**

Walter Foster Jr. titles are also available at discount for retail, wholesale, promotional, and bulk purchase. For details, contact the Special Sales Manager by email at specialsales@quarto.com or by mail at The Quarto Group, Attn: Special Sales Manager, 100 Cummings Center, Suite 265D, Beverly, MA 01915, USA.

ISBN: 978-0-7603-8074-1

Digital edition published in 2022
eISBN: 978-0-7603-8075-8

10 9 8 7 6 5 4 3 2 1

TABLE OF CONTENTS

Tools & Materials 4

Drawing Basics. 5

Bunny 8

Red Fox 12

Cow 16

Russian Dwarf Hamster 20

Red-Eared Slider Turtle 24

Llama 28

Squirrel 32

Giant Panda 36

Clydesdale Horse. 40

White-Tailed Deer .44

About the Author 48

TOOLS & MATERIALS

Welcome! You don't need much to start learning how to draw. Anyone can draw with just a pencil and piece of scrap paper, but if you want to get more serious about your art, additional artist's supplies are available.

PAPER If you choose printer paper, buy a premium paper that is thick enough and bright. Portable sketch pads keep all your drawings in one place, which is convenient. For more detailed art pieces, use a fine art paper.

PENCILS Standard No. 2 pencils and mechanical pencils are great to start with and inexpensive. Pencils with different graphite grades can be very helpful when shading because a specific grade (such as 4H, 2B, or HB) will only get so dark.

PENCIL SHARPENER Electric sharpeners are faster than manual ones, but they also wear down pencils faster. It's most economical to use an automatic one for inexpensive pencils and a manual sharpener for expensive ones.

ERASERS Some erasers can smear, bend, and even tear your paper, so get a good one that erases cleanly without smudges. Kneaded erasers are pliable and can be molded for precise erasing. They leave no residue, and they last a long time.

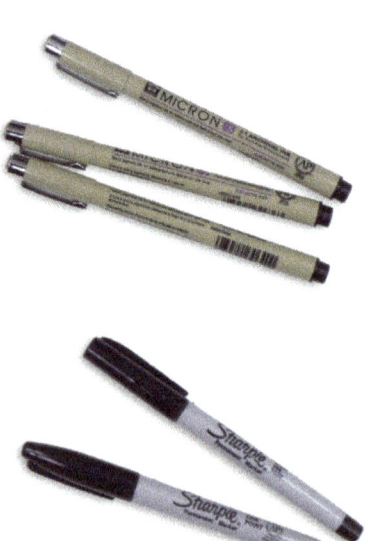

PENS If you want to outline a drawing after sketching it, you can use a regular Sharpie® pen or marker. For more intricate pieces, try Micron® pens, which come in a variety of tip thicknesses.

DRAWING BASICS

How to Draw Shapes

For the first steps of each project in this book, you will be drawing basic shapes as guide lines. Use light, smooth strokes and don't press down too hard with your pencil. If you sketch lightly at first, it will be easier to erase if you make a mistake.

You'll be drawing a lot of circles, which many beginning artists find difficult to create. These circles do not have to be perfect because they are just guides, but if you want to practice making better circles, try the four-marks method, as shown below.

1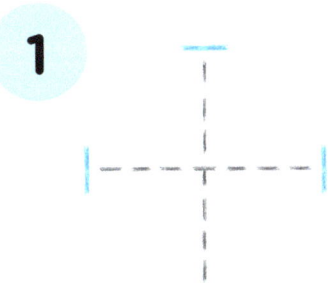

Mark where you want the top of the circle and, directly below, make another mark for the bottom. Do the same for the sides of the circle. If it helps, lightly draw a dotted line to help you place the other mark.

2

Once you have the four marks spaced apart equally, connect them using curved lines.

3

Erase any dotted lines you created, and you have a circle!

ADDITIONAL SHAPES While circles are usually what people find the most challenging, there are many other lines and shapes that you should practice and master. An arc can become a muzzle or tongue. Triangles can be ears, teeth, or claws. A football shape can become an eye. A curvy line can make a tail and an angled line a leg. Study the animal and note the shapes that stand out to you.

How to Shade

The final step to drawing an animal is to add shading so that it looks three-dimensional, and then adding texture so that it looks furry, feathery, smooth, or scaly. To introduce yourself to shading, follow the steps below.

1

Understand your pencil with a value scale. Using any pencil, start to shade lightly on one side and gradually darken your strokes toward the other side. This value scale will show you how light and dark your pencil can be.

2

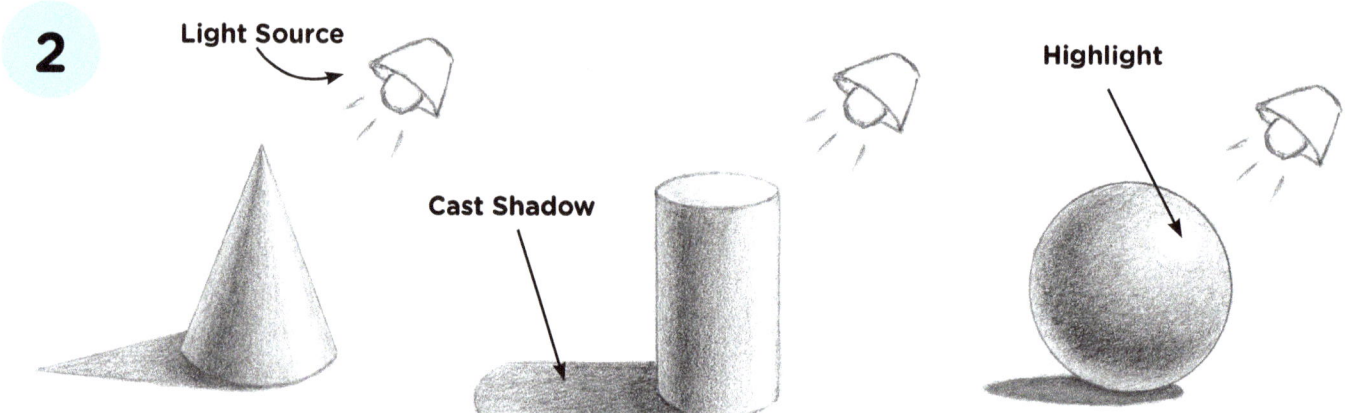

Light Source

Cast Shadow

Highlight

Apply the value scale to simple shapes. Draw simple shapes and shade them to make them look three-dimensional. Observe shadows in real life. Study how the light interacts with simple objects and creates shadows. Then try drawing what you see.

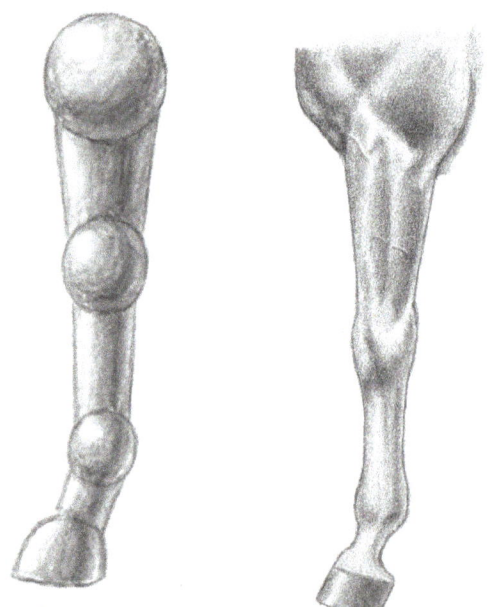

3

Practice with more complex objects. Once you're comfortable shading simple objects, move on to more complex ones. Note, for example, how a horse's leg is made up of cylinders and spheres. Breaking down your subject into simple shapes makes it easier to visualize the shadows.

How to Add Texture

Take what you've learned about shading one step further by adding texture to your drawings.

FURRY

One quick pencil stroke creates a single hair. Keep adding more quick, short strokes and you'll get a furry texture. Separate each individual stroke a bit so that the white of the paper comes through.

Create stripes and patterns by varying the pressure on your pencil to get different degrees of tonal value.

Make sure that your strokes follow the forms of the animal. As you shade a furry animal, use strokes that go in the general direction of the fur growth. The fur here follows the form of a simple sphere.

 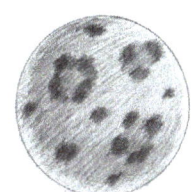

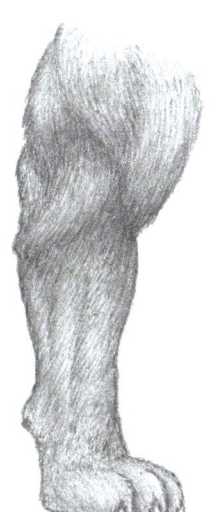

This is how to add fur to a complex form, which is easier if you know the animal's anatomy. In order to show the muscle structure, this image shows an exaggerated example of a lion's front leg and paw.

SMOOTH

For very short fur or smooth skin, add graphite evenly. Blend with a cotton swab, blending stump, or piece of tissue if needed.

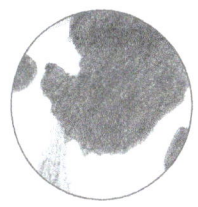

SCALY

For scaly animals like reptiles or dragons, create each individual scale with a tiny arc. Then add shadows to make the form look three-dimensional.

For a much easier way to get a scaly look, just add a bunch of squiggles! Make the squiggles darker in areas of pattern, as well as when adding shadows.

  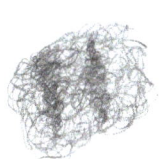 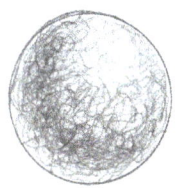

FEATHERED When adding texture to feathered animals, approach it as you would with fur or with smooth skin. Use a series of short strokes for fine or fluffy feathers. For smooth feathers, use even, blended value.

BUNNY

1 Draw two circles. One will be a guide for the bunny's body, and another will be for the head.

2 Add additional lines and arcs to create the muzzle, ears, back, chest, and leg. The line on the face will help you place the facial features later. Sketch these lines lightly at first so that it's easy to erase if you make a mistake.

3 Lightly sketch the eye on top of the construction line that you drew in the last step. When you get the size and placement right, darken the eye. Draw a couple of curved lines around the eye for extra detail.

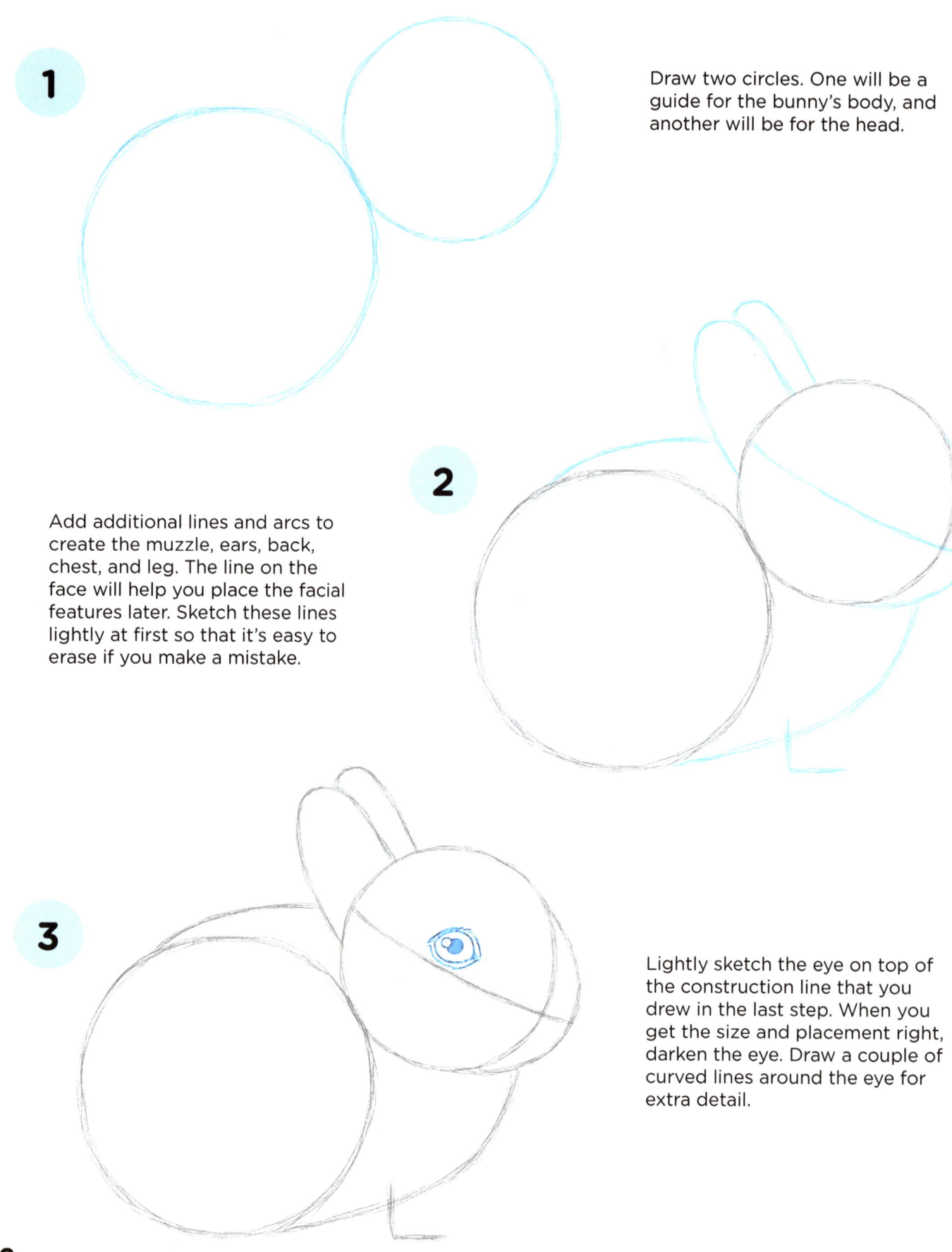

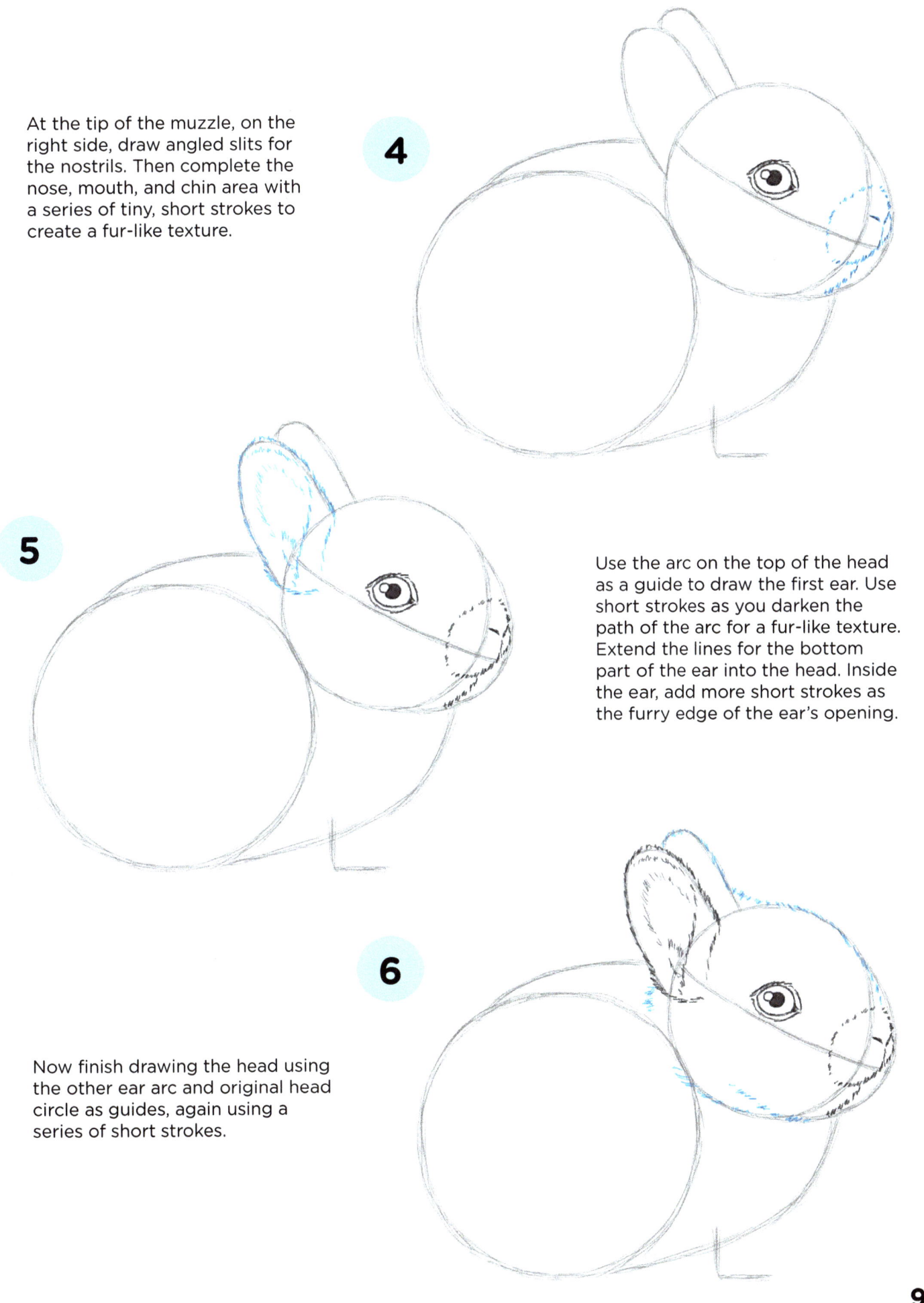

At the tip of the muzzle, on the right side, draw angled slits for the nostrils. Then complete the nose, mouth, and chin area with a series of tiny, short strokes to create a fur-like texture.

4

5

Use the arc on the top of the head as a guide to draw the first ear. Use short strokes as you darken the path of the arc for a fur-like texture. Extend the lines for the bottom part of the ear into the head. Inside the ear, add more short strokes as the furry edge of the ear's opening.

6

Now finish drawing the head using the other ear arc and original head circle as guides, again using a series of short strokes.

Follow the guides to draw the body and use a series of short strokes to create a furry texture. Make the strokes along the bottom of the body a bit longer. The longer you make these strokes, the shaggier the fur will appear.

7

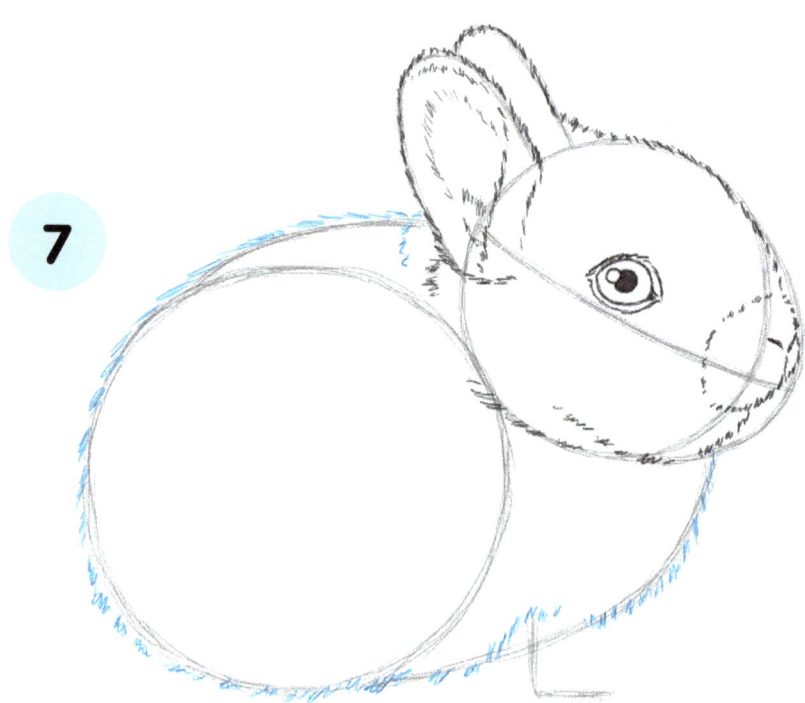

8

Use the angled line under the body as a guide to draw the first foot. Draw a couple of short, curved lines at the tip to separate the toes. Then use the first foot as a template to draw the other front foot. Finally, under the body, near the middle, draw a long, horizontal line that curves on the right for the hind foot. Because the bunny is sitting, the tail will not be visible.

SHADING Remember that shading can take a long time to complete, so be patient and take breaks. Slowly build up the value by adding strokes until you're happy with the result, and make sure to use pencil strokes that go in the general direction of the fur. Also separate each individual stroke a bit so that the white of the paper comes through, which creates a fur-like texture. It also requires a lot of practice to be able to shade well, so you may want to make a copy of your final sketch so you can try several times. Domestic rabbits can have a variety of different coats, so you can shade your drawing with different patterns.

9

For a cleaner look, erase as much as you can of the initial guide lines. Don't worry about erasing all of the guides. It's okay to leave some behind. Then re-draw any final sketch lines you may have accidentally erased.

10

Add some shadows to give the bunny more dimension and volume. Vary the pressure on your pencil to get different degrees of tonal value. Add a cast shadow underneath so it doesn't appear to be floating on the page. For a white bunny, stop after adding the shadows. For a gray bunny, add even more value throughout the body for extra detail. Make the muzzle a bit darker, and leave a few areas blank for white fur, like the edge of the ears, around the eye, and the bottom of the head and neck.

RED FOX

1

Draw a circle near the top of the paper as a guide for the fox's head. Draw a larger circle underneath and add another boxy shape under that. These shapes make the guide for the body.

2

Draw two curved lines and a circle inside the head. These will help you place the fox's facial features later. Add two triangle-like shapes as guides for the ears, two vertical lines for front legs, and two more lines on the bottom, one for the hind leg and one for the curved tail.

3

Sketch the eyes and nose using lines you drew in the last step as guides for placement. When drawing the nose, pay attention to all the little details in the image, and use short strokes at the top for the fur there. The eye on the right should be a bit bigger because of the perspective of the turned head.

4

Draw a long, wavy line under the nose for the mouth and another curved line under that for the fuzzy chin. Then create the fox's ears with quick, short strokes along the path of the triangle-like shapes. Add a few longer strokes within the ear for the fur found there and a few extra lines for structure.

5

Draw the rest of the head with quick, short strokes. The top of the head should be narrower than the initial circle. The bottom half should be wider and extend outside the main circle. Add a few more quick, short strokes within the head for a fur-like texture.

6

Draw the thin front legs. Add the paws at the bottom, with a few lines to separate the toes. On each toe, draw a small slit-like shape for the nails.

7

Using short strokes for a furry look, draw the body.

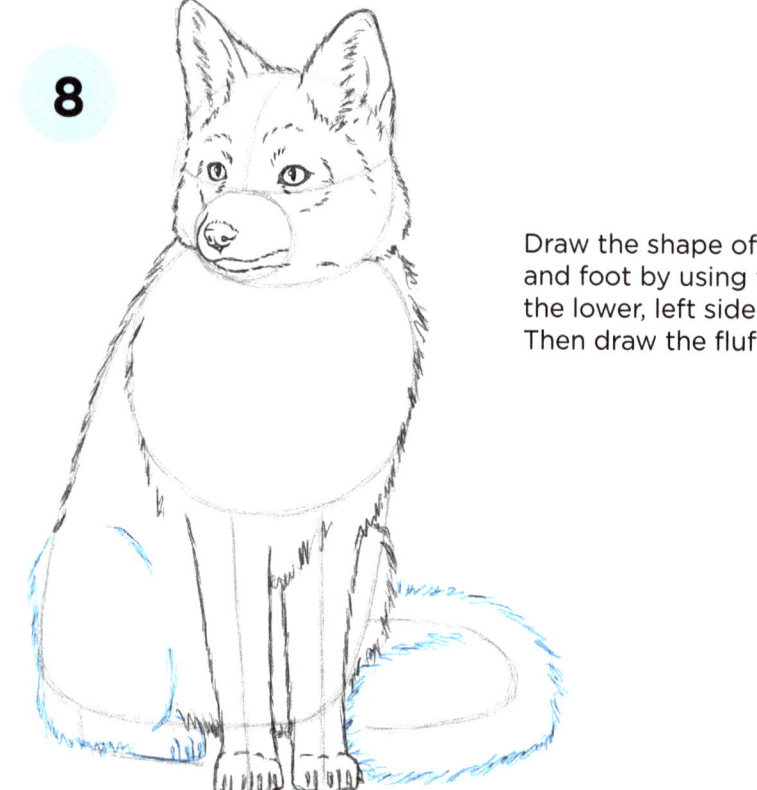

8

Draw the shape of the hind leg and foot by using the lines on the lower, left side as a guide. Then draw the fluffy, curved tail.

9

Tidy up your sketch. Erase the guide lines and re-draw any lines you'd like to fix.

ROUGH VALUE With furry animals, don't worry about shading too smoothly. A rough value will give the long coat a furry texture. Just remember to use strokes that go in the direction of the fur!

10

Use a dark value on the ears, nose, and side of the muzzle. Use a medium value for the top half of the head, leaving the bottom half (the cheeks) blank, and then continue to add a medium value to the body. Foxes have dark brown or black legs and feet, so use a dark value for them, too. Use a medium value for the tail, and if you'd like, add more value to the chest. Don't forget to add a cast shadow underneath.

15

COW

Lightly sketch three circles as guides for the cow's body and head. Add a U-shaped curve under the head for the muzzle.

1

Draw an arc on either side of the head as guides for the ears, two lines in the head shape to help place the facial features later on, and two lines under the body (one below each circle) as guides for the legs.

2

Connect the major shapes to form the body and add a long line on the right side for the tail.

3

4 Draw the eyes using the initial lines as guides for placement. Add waterdrop-shaped nostrils and a few lines around them for extra detail. Then use the U-shaped line as a guide to draw the mouth.

5 Create the ears and add a few more lines within them for extra detail. Then finish up the narrow head shape. Use quick, short strokes at the top of the head.

6 Using the lines as guides, draw a front and hind leg. The legs are thick on top and thin at the bottom. The hind leg is thicker at the base and angles back more. Be sure to draw a few bumps along the way to represent joints and the hooves at the bottom.

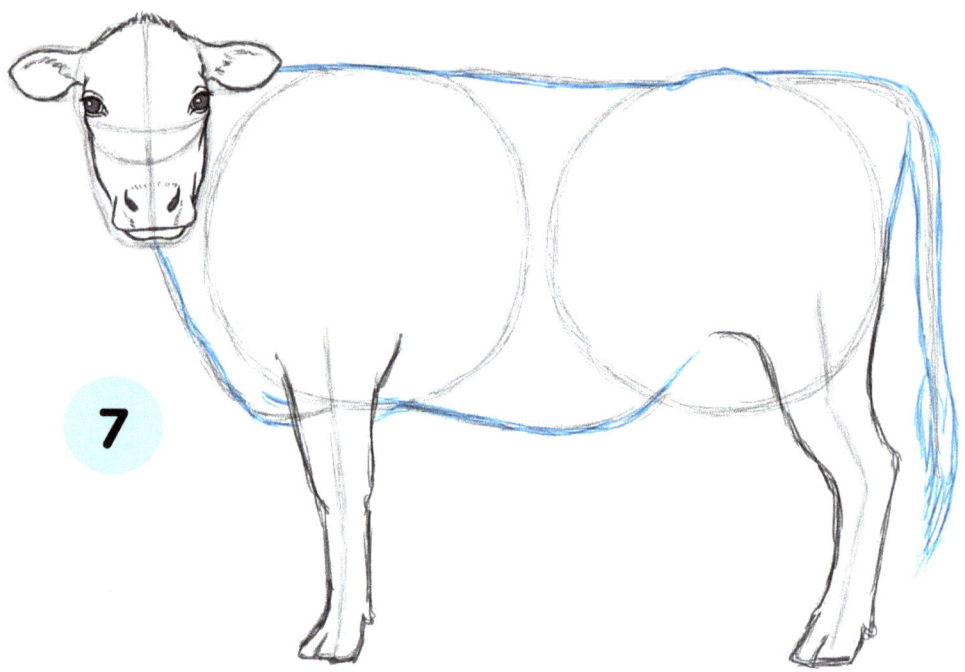

Darken the initial lines to draw the rest of the cow's body. Draw more curves and bumps along the way to give the body more structure. Add the tail on the right side with long strokes at the bottom for the hair found there.

7

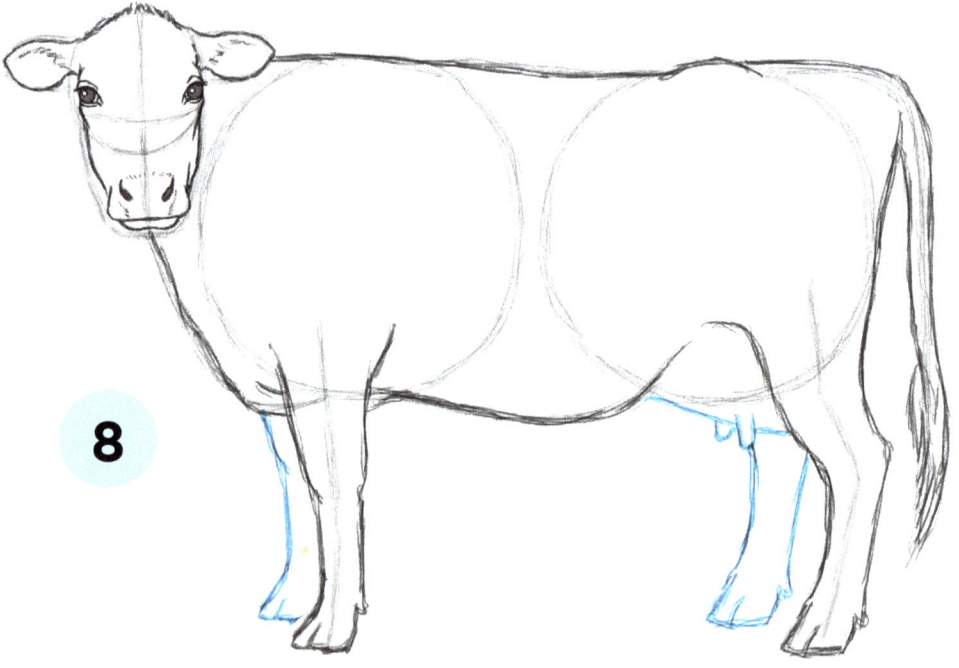

Draw the udder under the body on the right side, as well as the legs on the other side. Draw them the same way you did the first two.

8

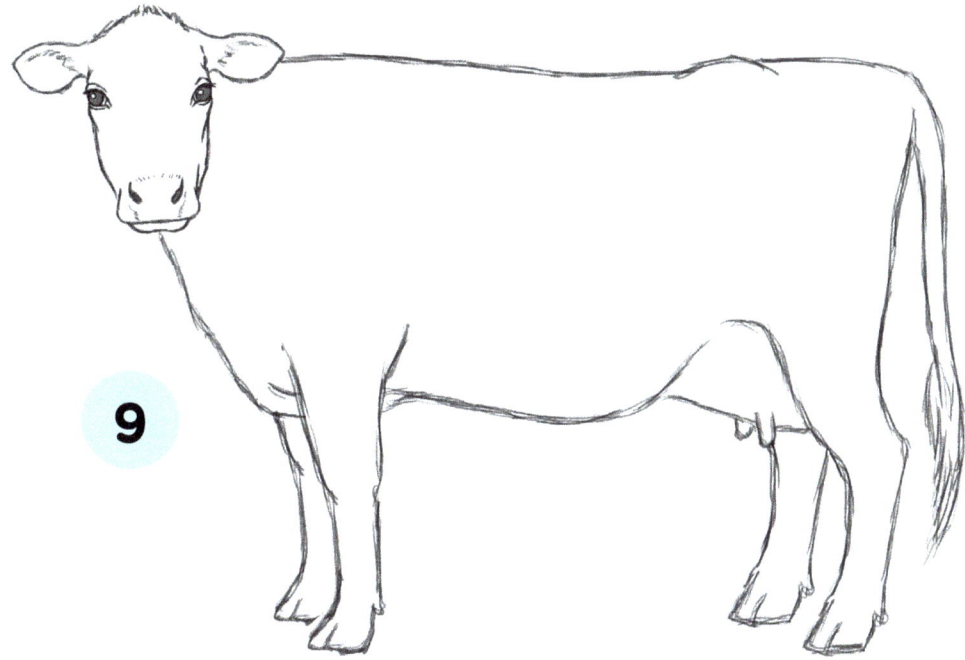

9

For a cleaner look, erase as much as you can of the initial guide lines. Don't worry about erasing all of them. It's OK to leave some behind. Also re-draw any final sketch lines that you may have accidentally erased.

10

Add some shading to your drawing to give it more dimension and volume, and include the cast shadow underneath the cow. For a Jersey cow, use a medium value all over the body. But for this classic Holstein pattern, draw dark patches throughout. You can use reference images when adding the markings on the body, but don't overthink it—just add the patches randomly.

RUSSIAN DWARF HAMSTER

Begin with two circles and two construction lines inside the head circle. Pay attention to the sizes and placement of the circles. If these guides are drawn correctly now, your hamster won't end up looking too short or long or thin or fat. It will look just right.

 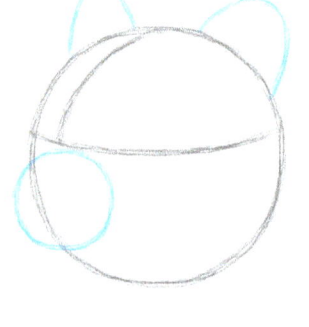 

On the left circle, draw a small circle as a guide for the muzzle and add two small arcs as guides for the ears.

Finish the guide for the body with additional curved lines. Then add three lines for feet and one on the right for the tail.

4

Lightly sketch the eyes. The eye on the left should be small and thin because the head is turned. When you get the eyes right, darken the shapes and add additional details. Then add the tiny nose with small lines.

EYES When drawing eyes, add a tiny circle (or in this case, two circles) off to the side for highlights. In the middle of the eye, draw a slightly bigger circle for the pupil. Shade the pupil using a dark value. When you shade the rest of the hamster's eye later on, don't overlap the small highlight circles. Use a dark value at the top and gradually make it lighter toward the bottom to give the eye a rounder look.

5

Around the nose, draw the top of the muzzle and the mouth. Then add a few dashed lines for the bases of the whiskers. Use the arcs as guides to draw the ears and add long strokes for the furry insides. The ear on the left is seen from the side, so draw a line for the edge of the ear and a series of strokes for fur on the left.

6

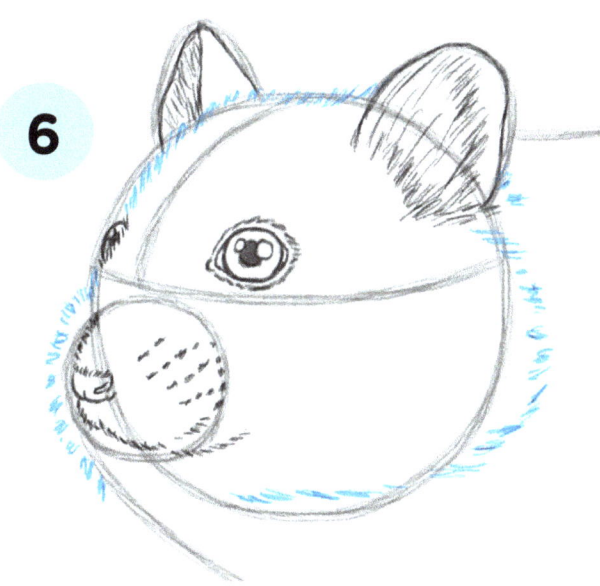

Use the big initial circle as a guide to draw the rest of the head. Note where to draw the lines inside and outside of the initial head circle.

Draw the visible feet. Draw four long toes on each foot, and then add the furry top parts of the feet.

7

Use the remaining lines and shapes as guides to draw the rest of the body. Make your pencil strokes short near the head and longer on the body. Add the triangular tail on the right.

8

Either leave your drawing as a sketch or, for a cleaner look, erase as much as you can of the initial guide lines and tidy up your drawing.

9

10

Shade your dwarf hamster lightly at first and gradually build up to darker values. As you shade the head, use strokes that radiate outward from the nose. Leave the bottom of the head and the muzzle white. Alternate between dark and light value on the top part of the body and use a very light value on the bottom half. Add strokes with a medium value along the bottom for shadows and add a cast shadow underneath the hamster. Use smoother shading for the feet and tail because they aren't furry.

RED-EARED SLIDER TURTLE

1

First draw some shapes to create guides for the small head and large shell.

2

Add an arc to the head. Then connect the head to the body with lines. Sketch angled lines for legs and a triangle-like shape for the tail, and you now have all of your basic shapes done. You can begin adding the details!

3

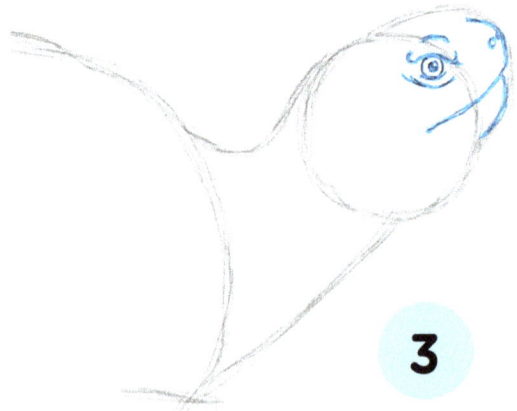

Draw the eye as a circle with a pupil and highlight circle inside. Add a series of lines around the eye for detail. The lines give the head a bumpier texture. Then draw the mouth using curved lines. Small circles make up the nose.

4

Use the initial lines as guides to draw the rest of the head and neck. Avoid using straight lines and make sure to add a bump near the top to hint at the eye that's on the other side of the head. Then draw a curvy shape next to the eye to represent the red portion of the head.

5

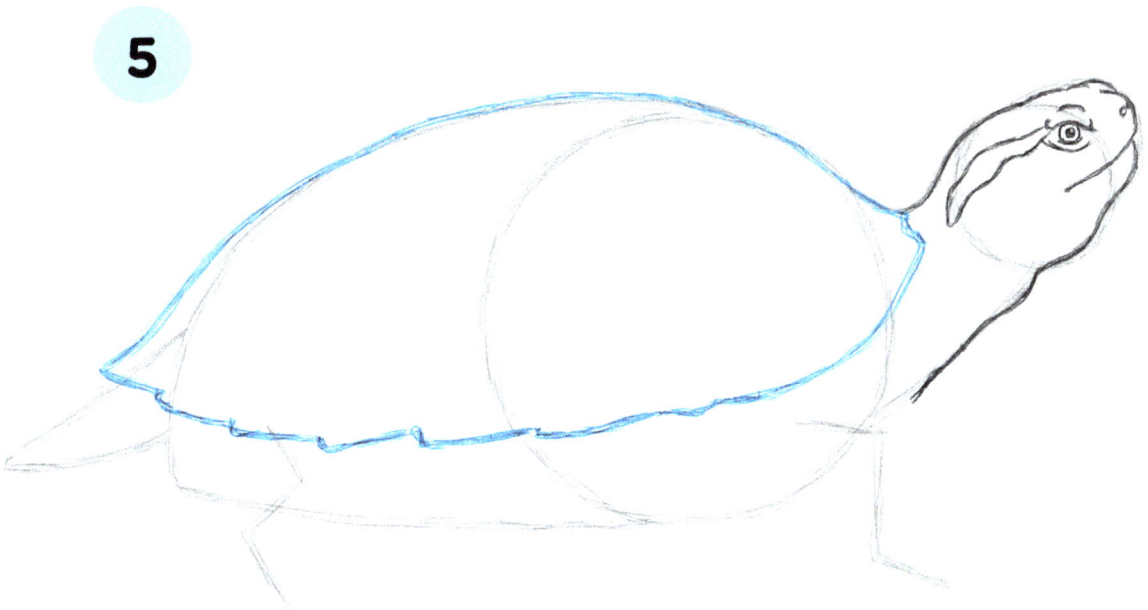

Sketch the shape of the shell. While the top is a smooth line, use jagged lines at the bottom to indicate the rough edge.

6

Use the angled lines to draw the legs and feet. Note all of the angles and curves. You are also drawing the bottom shell openings in this step. Finally, add small triangles on the toes for the claws.

7

Begin drawing the shapes within the shell with a row of square-like shapes at the bottom of the shell.

8

Finish the shell with larger pentagon-like shapes and lines. Then add the bottom part of the shell and use the small triangle on the left as a guide to draw the tail.

9

Stop here for a sketch or tidy up your drawing to add shading in the next step.

10

Give your red-eared slider turtle drawing more dimension and volume with shading. Also add a cast shadow underneath. Then add more value throughout, including the stripes and spots on the body, as well as the pattern on the shell.

LLAMA

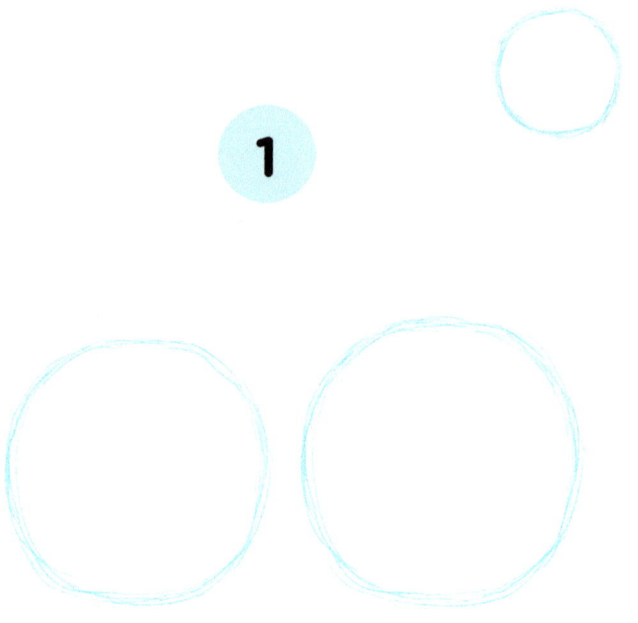

1

Draw two circles as guides for the llama's body and a smaller circle at the top, right. Notice the spacing between the circles.

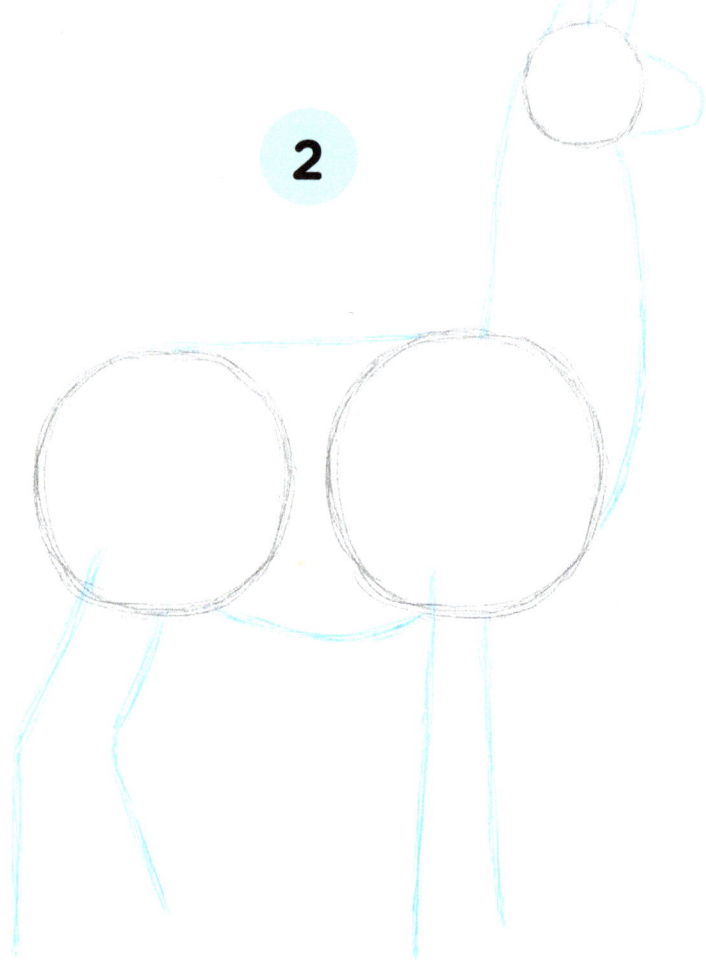

2

Finish the guide lines in this step. Add the ears, muzzle, neck, body, and leg lines. Once these lines look good to you, it's time to move on to the face.

3

There are a lot of little lines and curves that make up the eye and mouth. Pay close attention to the reference image to make sure you get them all down on your paper.

4

Add the ears using the M shape on top of the head as a guide. Darken the shape of the ear on the left and have it extend down inside the head circle a bit. Then use quick, short strokes within the shape to represent fur. Draw the other ear, which is viewed from the side.

5

Use quick, short strokes throughout the face to give it a furry look.

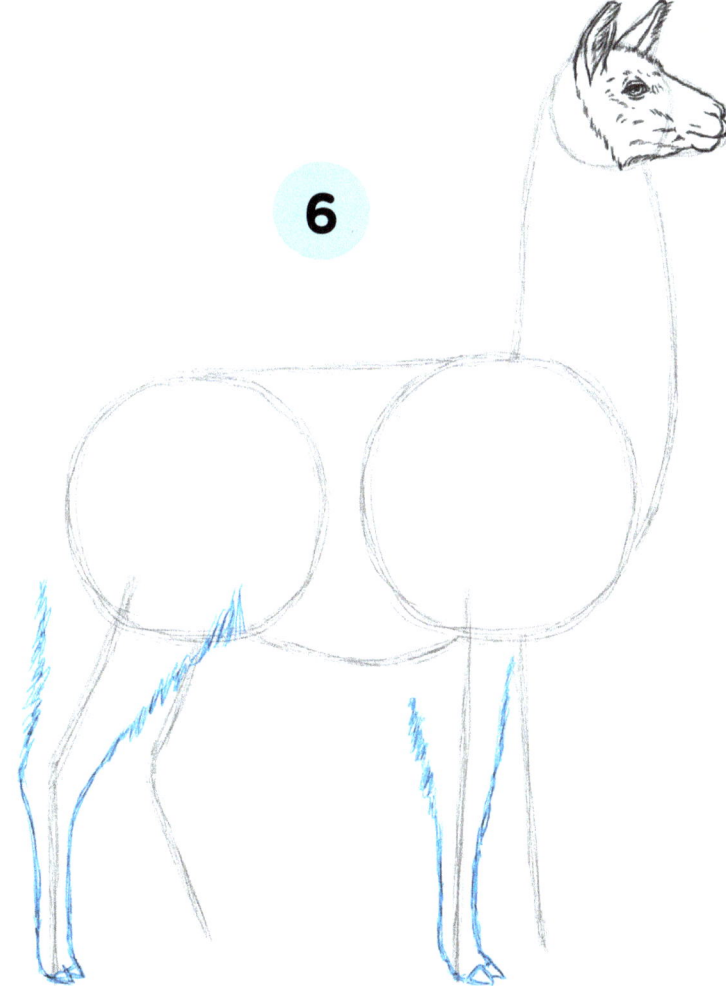

6

Draw the first two legs, using quick, short strokes at the top for fur. Draw the two toes at the bottom as triangles.

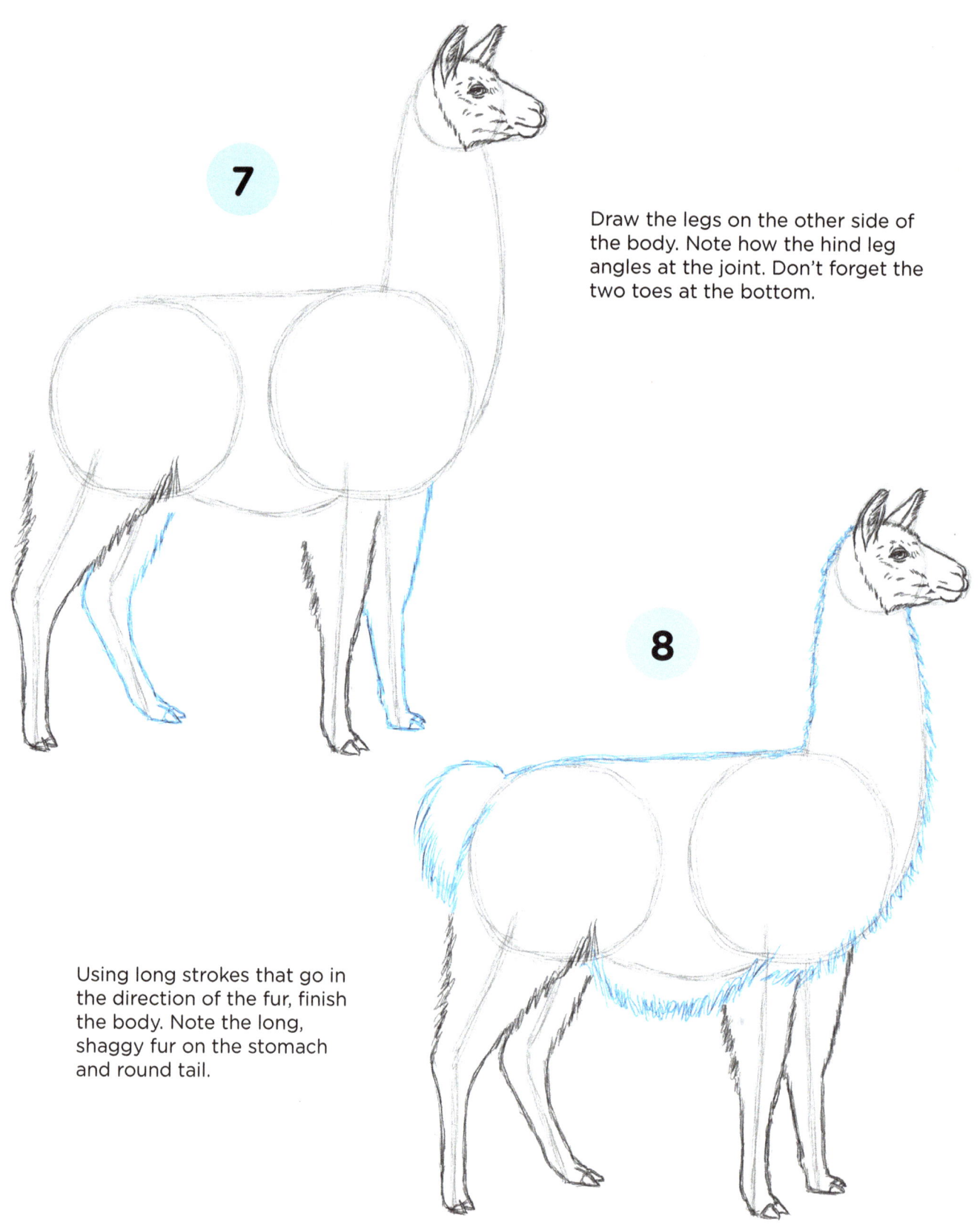

7

Draw the legs on the other side of the body. Note how the hind leg angles at the joint. Don't forget the two toes at the bottom.

8

Using long strokes that go in the direction of the fur, finish the body. Note the long, shaggy fur on the stomach and round tail.

DIMENSION & VOLUME To make a two-dimensional drawing look three-dimensional, decide where the light source should be and create shadows where they would appear in real life. Adding accurate shadows to drawings takes time and practice to do well, so for now, observe your references (in this case, the final step) and copy what you see, taking note where the shadows are.

9

Tidy up your drawing by erasing guide lines and re-drawing anything that you'd like to fix before shading.

10

With long strokes for the fur, add shading that goes in the direction of the fur growth. Note the darker areas where shadows are darker. Finally, add a cast shadow underneath the llama, and you're done!

SQUIRREL

1 First draw two circles that overlap each other, as well as an arc coming off the smaller circle.

2 Add two arcs for ears, a horizontal line across the head shape, a line for the neck, and an arc that turns the body circle into an oval shape.

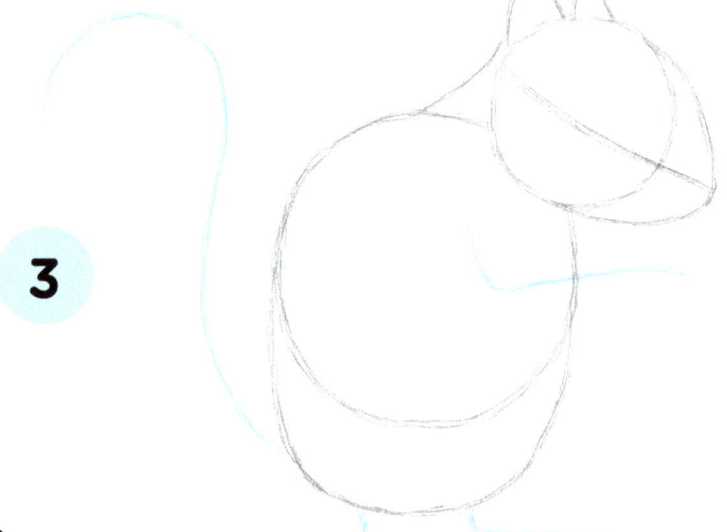

3 Finish up your guide lines with lines for the limbs and a long, curved line for the tail.

4

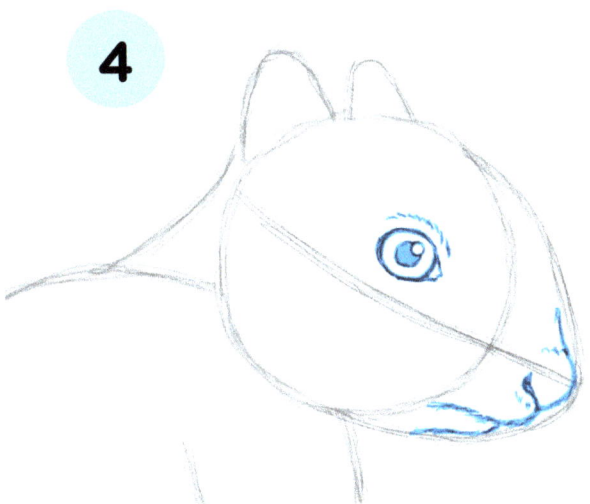

Draw the eye using the line in the center to help with placement. Add the inner corner of the eye and short strokes above it for detail. Then add the nose and mouth with curved lines and short strokes for additional details.

5

Use the arcs to draw the ears, adding details inside the one on the left. With quick, short strokes to represent the fur, finish the head.

6

Use the initial lines as guides to draw two of the limbs. Use quick, short strokes for the fur and include curved lines at the ends for the digits.

7 Draw what's visible of the other two limbs, as well as a nut in the front paws.

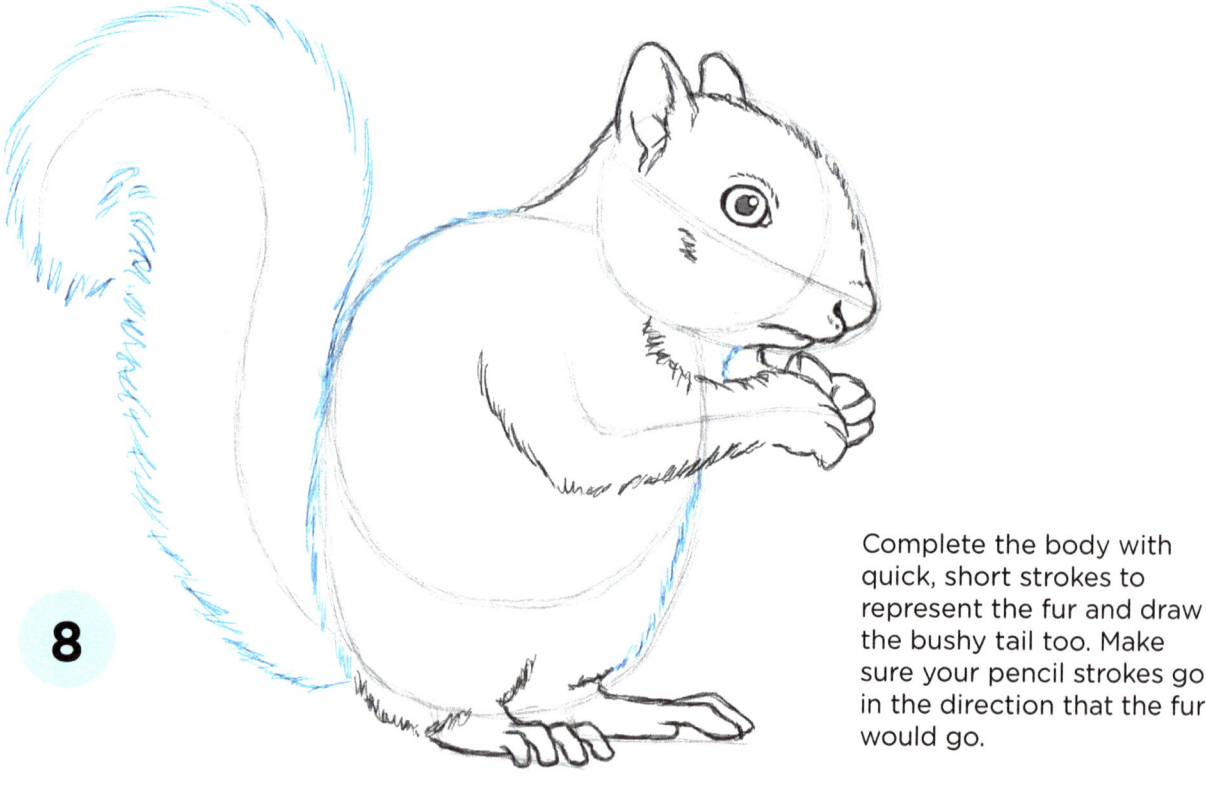

8 Complete the body with quick, short strokes to represent the fur and draw the bushy tail too. Make sure your pencil strokes go in the direction that the fur would go.

9

For a cleaner look, erase as much as you can of the initial guide lines and re-draw anything you'd like to fix.

Add some shadows on the squirrel and a cast shadow underneath. Use a medium-to-dark value on the body, but leave some areas lighter, including around the eye, cheeks, neck, and underside. Make sure your strokes go in the general direction of the fur, and leave some space between each pencil stroke so the white of the paper shows through.

10

GIANT PANDA

1

The guides for the panda look a little bit like a snowman that's flat on the bottom and leaning to the side.

Draw two intersecting lines inside the head. These are construction lines that will help you place the panda's facial features later on. Then add circles, which will be guides for the paws.

2

3

Draw a small circle in the head for the muzzle, two arcs on the head for the ears, and lines that connect the body to the paw circles for the limbs.

4

Sketch the eyes and nose. Don't worry too much about the eyes because the patches you'll draw around them later will make them hard to see, but don't draw them too big. Pandas have small eyes.

5

Draw a thick, dark, horizontal line under the nose for the mouth. Then use quick, short strokes along the small circle guide to create the muzzle and chin.

6

Now create the fuzzy head and ears.

7

With furry strokes, draw the panda's arms or front limbs. Note where you should use longer and shorter strokes for the fur of different lengths.

8

Add the hind legs the same way.

9

In this step, add five triangle-like claws to each paw and quick, short strokes for the furry bases. Then draw paw pads on the bottom feet.

10

Finish drawing the rest of the panda's body with quick, short strokes along the outer edges of the guides to create the fur-like texture. Add some quick, short strokes on the chest.

11

Erase as much as you can of the initial guide lines and clean up your sketch so it is ready for shading.

MAKE IT DIFFERENT You can also turn this panda drawing into a grizzly bear or black bear by adding a medium value all over the body.

12

Start by outlining where the dark fur will be: around the ears, eyes, and limbs. Then add a dark value to these areas, being careful not to add value in the claws. Use a slightly lighter value for the padding on the feet. Add a bit of light value to the white sections as well. This value creates shadows and gives the panda dimension and volume. Add a cast shadow underneath, and your panda is complete!

CLYDESDALE HORSE

1

Start with three circles. Pay attention to the distance between the circles or your horse might end up looking like a giraffe!

2

Add a U-shaped arc for the muzzle, a triangle-like shape for the ears, and four lines under the body (two below each circle) as guides for the legs. One front leg will be raised as the horse steps forward, so this line should bend in two places and be shorter.

3

Draw lines that will connect the head and body, and add a line for the tail on the right.

4

Lightly sketch the eye and nose and darken the lines when you're happy with what you've drawn. Add a few lines around the eye for the detail on the folds of skin.

5

With a series of curved lines, draw the rest of the nose and mouth area. Then use the triangle on top of the head to create the ears. Extend the lines for the base of the first ear in toward the head a bit more. Draw some smaller lines on the left for the tip of the other ear.

6

Between the ears, draw the forelock as a clump, rather than making every individual hair strand. Finish the head, making it a bit narrower than the guides, especially the bottom. Add a curved line on the right for the strong jaw and a series of lines within the head to give it more structure.

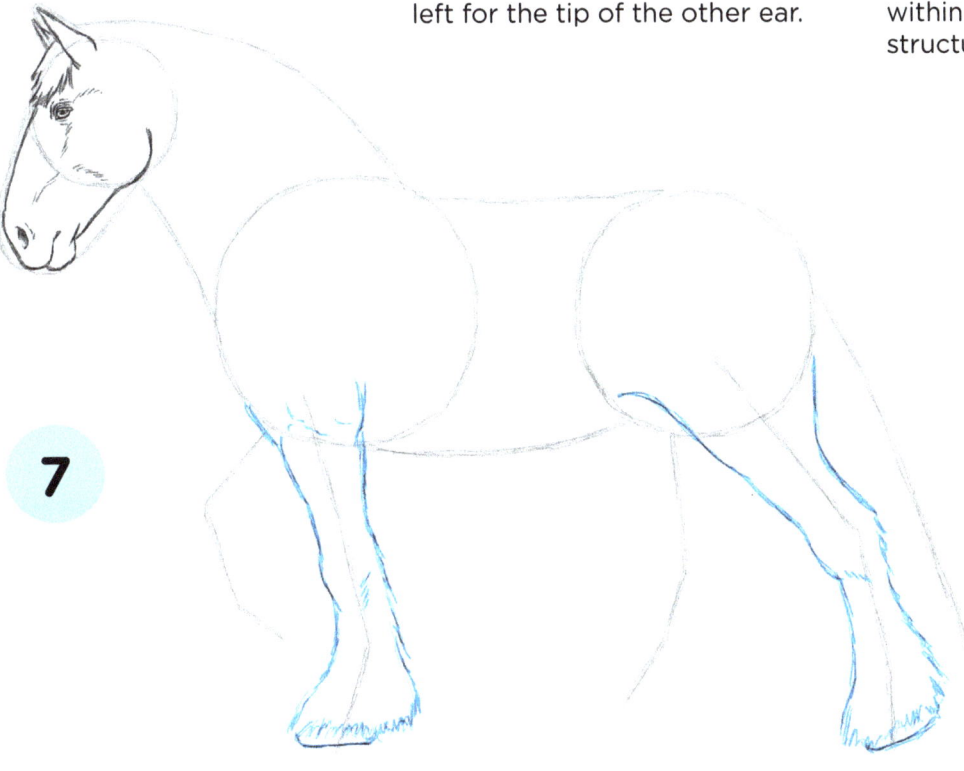

7

Draw one front leg and one hind leg. Use curved lines as you darken the shape to represent the joints and muscle structure of the leg. Then draw the visible portion of the hoof at the bottom.

NOTING DIFFERENCES While all horses have a similar structure, there are noticeable differences between the breeds. Clydesdale and shire horses have very thick, muscular legs compared to Arabians, for example, so make this horse's legs thick. As you darken the bottoms, make the shape wider to represent the extra hair called "feathers" found on this breed. Use a series of quick, short strokes along the bottom edge to represent the tips of the feathers.

Add the mane and tail with quick, short pencil strokes. Just like you would when drawing human hair, draw the overall shape of the hair and not every individual hair strand.

8

Finish the horse's body with curved lines.

9

Complete the legs on the other side of the body following the legs you already drew as templates. The horse is stepping forward, so bend the front leg's shape and lift it up off the ground.

10

Stop here for a sketch or clean up your drawing to prepare it for shading.

11

12

Add some shading to give your Clydesdale more dimension and volume and to emphasize its muscle structure. Don't forget to add a cast shadow so it won't appear to be floating. Add a dark value with vertical strokes as you shade the mane, leaving a lighter value across the middle part to represent shine. Leave the front of the head and the bottoms of the legs white, and use a medium value for the rest of the body. Use a light value along the back and rump to give the coat a nice sheen. Try to add the value evenly for a smooth coat.

WHITE-TAILED DEER

1

Draw three circles as guides for the body and head. Note their sizes and placement.

2

Add three arcs on the head for the ears and muzzle, two curved lines inside the head to help you place the eyes later on, and three lines under the body for the legs.

Finish your guide lines with lines that connect the body and head, as well as two curved lines on the head as guides for the antlers.

3

GUIDE LINES Remember to sketch in guide lines lightly, and don't worry if your circles aren't perfect. Turn back to page 5 to refresh your memory on how to draw a circle. You will erase guide lines later on, so instead of worrying about making a perfect circle, focus more on its size and placement in relation to the rest of the shapes.

4

Add the eyes and large nose to the face. Note the shape of the eye on the left.

5

Draw the antlers. The initial guides act as the bottom of the antlers, so just draw a few more spikes on top.

6

Draw the rest of the muzzle and head. Note where the lines look smooth (above the nose) and where they are furry (on the jaw and chin).

7

Finish the head by drawing the ears.

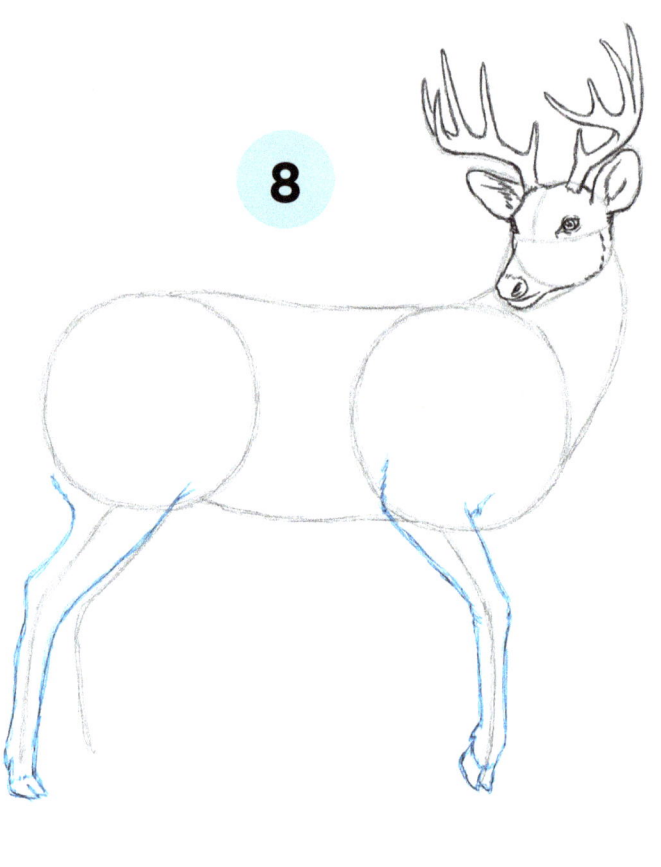

8

Draw the lifted front leg. Sketch lightly at first, darkening your lines when you're satisfied with them. Use curved lines to bend the leg and draw bumps at the joints. Add the hoof at the bottom. Draw the hind leg the same way, but make it wider at the top.

9

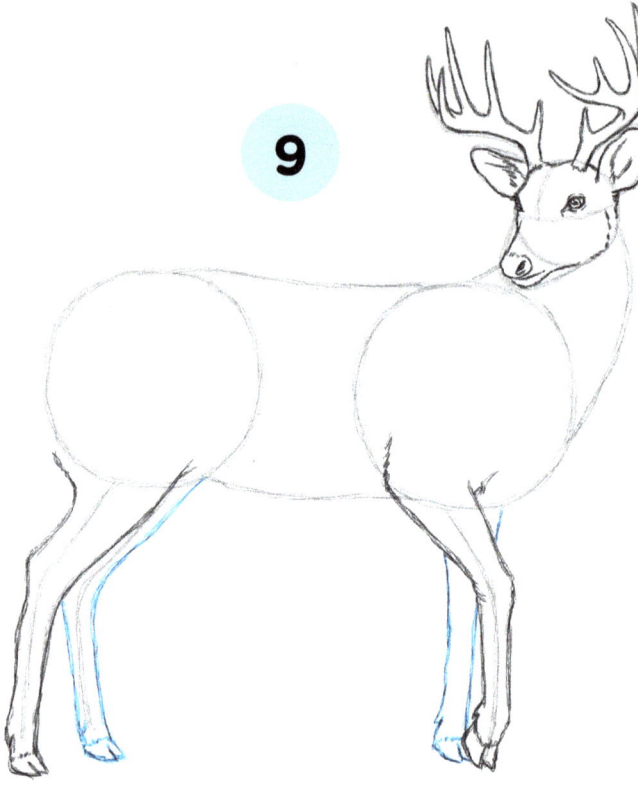

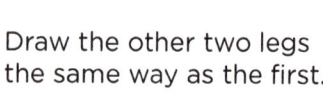

Draw the other two legs the same way as the first.

10

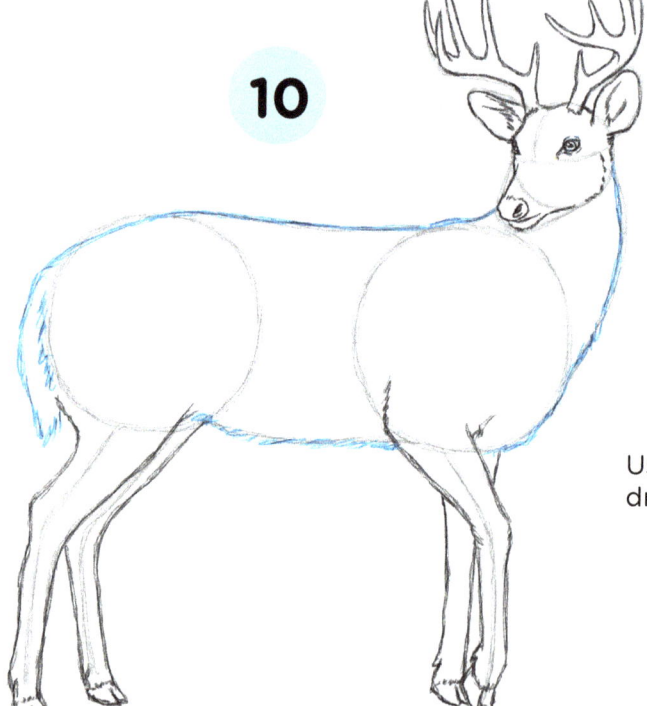

Use the rest of the guides to draw the body and tail.

Erase your guide lines and clean up your drawing so you can begin shading.

11

Shade to define the deer's muscles, add structure, and to indicate the areas of light and dark on the fur. Don't forget to add a cast shadow underneath.

12

ABOUT THE AUTHOR

How2DrawAnimals.com teaches beginning artists how to draw all kinds of animals from A to Z through video demonstrations and simple step-by-step instructions. Started in 2012 by an animal-loving artist with a bachelor's degree in illustration, How2DrawAnimals offers a new tutorial each week and now boasts hundreds of animal drawing tutorials. Working in graphite and in colored pencils, and in both realistic and cartoon styles, How2DrawAnimals has featured animals from all letters of the alphabet, from Aardvark to Zebra and everything in between. See more at How2DrawAnimals.com.

ALSO IN THE LET'S DRAW SERIES:

Let's Draw Cats
ISBN: 978-0-7603-8070-3

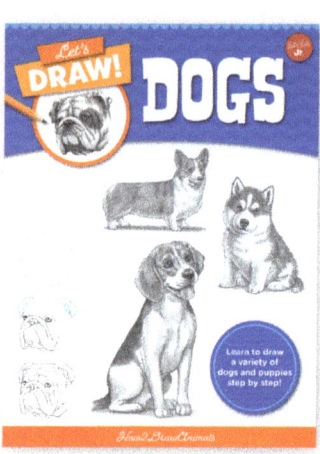

Let's Draw Dogs
ISBN: 978-0-7603-8072-7

Let's Draw Wild Animals
ISBN: 978-0-7603-8076-5

Let's Draw Birds & Butterflies
ISBN: 978-0-7603-8078-9

Let's Draw Sea Creatures
ISBN: 978-0-7603-8080-2

Let's Draw Dinosaurs
ISBN: 978-0-7603-8082-6

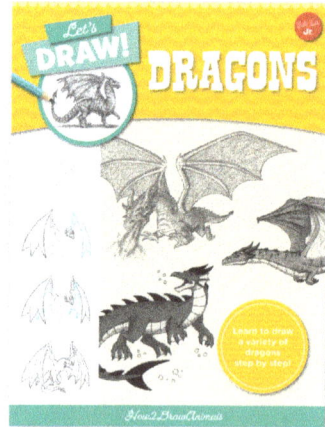

Let's Draw Dragons
ISBN: 978-0-7603-8084-0

Inspiring | Educating | Creating | Entertaining

www.WalterFoster.com

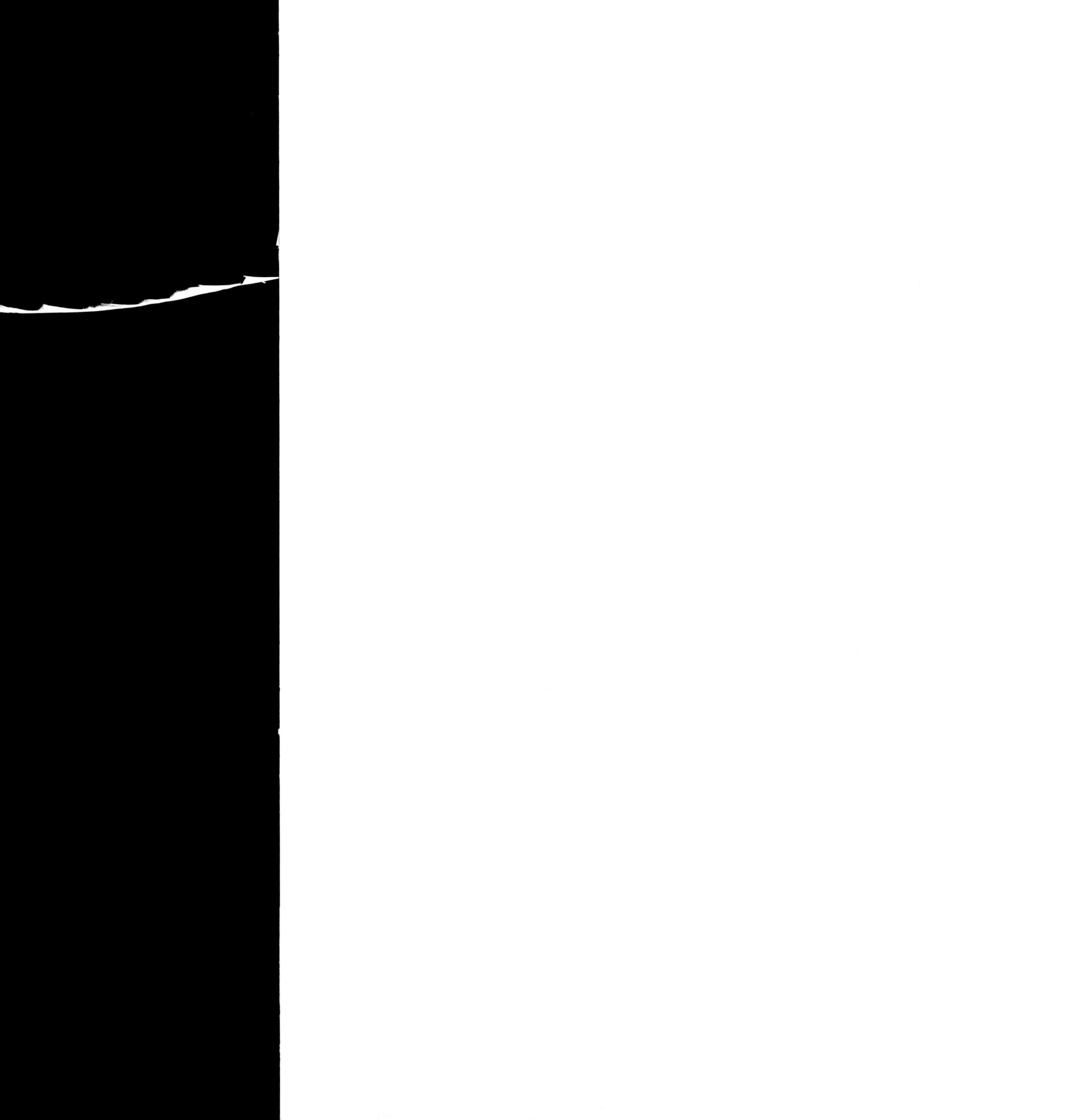